Heroes for Young Readers

Written by Renee Taft Meloche
Illustrated by Bryan Pollard

Adoniram Judson	Gladys Aylward
Amy Carmichael	Hudson Taylor
Bethany Hamilton	Ida Scudder
Betty Greene	Jim Elliot
Brother Andrew	Jonathan Goforth
Cameron Townsend	Loren Cunningham
Corrie ten Boom	Lottie Moon
C. S. Lewis	Mary Slessor
David Livingstone	Nate Saint
Eric Liddell	Nick Vujicic
George Müller	William Carey

Heroes of History for Young Readers

Written by Renee Taft Meloche
Illustrated by Bryan Pollard

Daniel Boone
Clara Barton
George Washington
George Washington Carver
Louis Zamperini
Meriwether Lewis

*Heroes for Young Readers Activity Guides and audio CDs
are also available. See the back of this book for more information.*

www.HeroesThenAndNow.com

HEROES FOR YOUNG READERS

NATE SAINT

Heavenbound

Written by Renee Taft Meloche
Illustrated by Bryan Pollard

Nate Saint: Heavenbound   Text © 2001 by Renee Taft Meloche   Illustrations © 2001 by Bryan Pollard
Published by YWAM Publishing, P.O. Box 55787, Seattle, WA 98155   ISBN 978-1-57658-229-9   Printed in China.   All rights reserved.

Sitting in a biplane was
    a boy whose name was Nate.
This airplane ride would be his first
    and he could hardly wait.

The pilot was his brother Sam.
    The engine noise grew loud.
Nate thought, *What will it soon be like
    to be among the clouds?*

The big propeller spun and whirled.
    The plane prepared to fly.
It soon sped down the runway and
    then lifted toward the sky.

Nate's heart beat fast with joy as he
    could feel the chilly air.
It filled the open cockpit and
    blew right through his brown hair.

Nate lived in Philadelphia,
    and soon his plane had flown
so very high up in the sky
    a dot was now his home.

Three years passed by and Nate went on
     his second airplane ride.
The plane was built so he and Sam
     could now sit side by side.

Once they were off, Sam turned to Nate,
     "You want to fly it now?"
Nate nodded as he took the wheel,
     though he was not sure how.

He pulled back on the wheel and sent
     the airplane heavenbound.
He pushed it forward and its nose
     dipped quickly toward the ground.

It felt just like a roller coaster
and there was no doubt
that Nate would be a pilot since
that's all he talked about.

When Nate grew up he learned to fly.
  He also prayed and thought,
I'd like to be a pilot who
  could serve the Lord a lot.

He learned about some very brave
  and fearless men who flew.
They took their planes through jungles that
  were scary flying through.

These men helped Christians overseas
  to teach about their Lord,
so Nate flew with his family to
  the country Ecuador.

Nate flew supplies to missionaries
  who were living there,
where Nate and his small yellow plane
  became a welcome pair.

Nate stored supplies in hollow tubes
    upon the airplane's wings,
then pulled a cord which opened up
    a hatch that dropped the things.

Supplies were dropped by parachute,
    and once these goods would land
they all were picked up gratefully
    by eager, waiting hands.

Once Nate dropped down a bucket with
    a telephone in it.
A missionary picked it up
    and said, "We need help quick!
Some villagers are very sick."
    Nate flew off straightaway
and then returned with medicine,
    which helped save lives that day.

The years passed by, then in the fall
    of nineteen fifty-five,
Nate flew where few outsiders had
    come out of there alive.

A friend named Ed flew with him to
    this most unfriendly place,
where one tribe lived that others feared
    and did not want to face.

For when priests or explorers would
    come visit day or night,
they often were attacked although
    they had not come to fight.

Outsiders called them Aucas, though
    Waorani was their name.
This Auca word meant "savage" since
    they speared all those who came.

Nate longed to let the Aucas hear
　　the good news of God's Son,
and show them how God loved them and
　　the great things He had done.

But first Nate had to be their friend.
　　He'd do his best and try.
He thought, *I'll drop the Aucas gifts
　　from up here in the sky.*

So Nate and Ed flew near the shore
　　and found a sandy spot.
They dropped a kettle down in hopes
　　that they would find the pot.

Nate flew his yellow Piper plane
　　around the shore again,
then spotted lots of Auca men
　　now waving up at them!

A cloth was wrapped around their waists.
    Their hair was thick and black.
Ed wanted to make friends with them
    and knew he had to act.

He lowered down a bucket at
    the end of one long rope.
It blew into the water, though,
    which gave him little hope.

Then one brave Auca dived right in
    before it went adrift.
Inside it was a great big knife,
    a very useful gift.

The Auca wildly waved the knife
  up high above his head.
A smile spread across his face,
  which pleased both Nate and Ed.

When Nate returned, the Aucas all
  looked up as he flew near.
Nate spoke words in their language through
  a speaker loud and clear.

As Nate kept dropping gifts to them,
  they also sent a few:
a headdress, monkey's tail and
  a talking parrot too.

Now on their eighth trip Ed yelled out,
    "We want to come near you!"
The Aucas danced and raised their hands
    as their excitement grew.

As Nate looked at the scene below,
    his eyes scanned left and right.
He had to find an open space
    to be his landing site.

He skimmed his plane down lower and
    then spied a place to land.
It was both wide and very straight,
    a beach with pure white sand.

So Nate flew Ed and three more friends
        back to that sandy beach,
to share God's love with Aucas that
        they prayed and hoped to reach.

The men soon set to work and made
        a treehouse out of wood,
so they could sleep when nighttime came
        as safely as they could.

Nate flew to where the Aucas lived
        and soon told everyone
that they now lived nearby and were
        invited all to come.

Returning to the beach, Nate joined
        the missionaries there.
They listened, watched, and waited and
        they spent much time in prayer.

Yet not one single Auca came.
        Instead each noise they heard
turned out to be some animal
        or noisy jungle bird.

Then after two long days Nate heard
    a rustling in the trees.
Two Auca women then stepped out.
    The men were greatly pleased.

They gently led both women to
    a campsite in the shade,
and as the women settled down,
    they poured them lemonade.

Then soon an Auca man appeared,
    quite muscular and small.
The missionaries named him George.
    He showed no fear at all.

He climbed into the airplane so
    Nate took him for a trip.
George stared in wonder as the plane
    flew straight and then would dip.

Nate circled round the village as
    they both enjoyed the view.
George laughed to see the looks of shock
    from people that he knew.

Not knowing it was dangerous,
    George crawled onto the wing.
Nate pulled him back and landed and
    then brought out fun-filled things:
a yo-yo and harmonica,
    balloons and other toys.
The day was clearly going well.
    Nate felt a sense of joy.

As darkness fell the younger woman
    ran off in the night.
George liked her so he followed her,
    yet knew it was not right.

For he'd been taught that someone else
    should keep an eye on them.
Young women who weren't married should
    not be alone with men.

The next day George came up with an
    excuse before his tribe:
"The white men all attacked us but
    we got away," he lied.
"The younger woman and myself
    were left there on our own.
That's why the two of us both had
    to spend the night alone."

This made the Aucas angry at
    the white men in the end.
They now believed the white men did
    not want to be their friends.

That afternoon six Aucas left
    the campground with their spears.
They headed toward the river as
    they silently grew near.

They crouched down low and swiftly moved
    beneath the morning light.
They closed in on the white men till
    they had them in their sights.

The Aucas crept up from behind
    but then their leader slipped.
He fell down off a long wet log,
    which made him lose his grip.

The spears their leader carried all
    came crashing to the ground.
The missionaries heard the noise
    and quickly turned around.

Their leader grabbed his weapon and
    he cried a warrior's yell,
drew back his arm, then threw his spear,
    and when he did Nate fell.

As Ed rushed over to his side,
    a sharp spear pierced his skin,
and just like that the Aucas had
    killed Nate and then killed him.

In minutes it was over and
    five men of God were dead.
They'd hoped to bring the Aucas love
    but met with hate instead.

Days later when the news had spread
        that all the men had died,
their families' hearts were broken and
        for days and weeks they cried.

It was almost impossible
        to think that any good
could come from what had happened, yet
        with God it really would.

Nate had a sister Rachel and
        she loved the Aucas too.
She'd learned the Auca language through
        a woman that she knew.

Two Auca women came to her
        inviting her to stay
and live among the Auca tribe
        and learn about their ways.

Some members of the tribe thought she
    might try to get them back:
because they'd killed her brother she
    might plan her own attack.

Yet Rachel had forgiven them,
    though Nate's death made her sad.
"I'll show God's love to you," she said.
    "It's true that I'm not mad."

Just six years after Nate was killed
        because of George's lies,
some Aucas became Christians which
        was quite a great surprise!

Nate loved the Auca Indians and
        he also loved his Lord.
And he lives on in heaven now.
        How great is his reward!

Heroes for Young Readers and *Heroes of History for Young Readers are based on the Christian Heroes: Then & Now and Heroes of History biographies by Janet & Geoff Benge. Don't miss out on these exciting, true adventures for ages 10 and up!*

Christian Heroes: Then & Now
by Janet & Geoff Benge

Adoniram Judson: Bound for Burma
Amy Carmichael: Rescuer of Precious Gems
Betty Greene: Wings to Serve
Brother Andrew: God's Secret Agent
Cameron Townsend: Good News in Every Language
Clarence Jones: Mr. Radio
Corrie ten Boom: Keeper of the Angels' Den
Count Zinzendorf: Firstfruit
C. S. Lewis: Master Storyteller
C. T. Studd: No Retreat
David Bussau: Facing the World Head-on
David Livingstone: Africa's Trailblazer
Dietrich Bonhoeffer: In the Midst of Wickedness
D. L. Moody: Bringing Souls to Christ
Elisabeth Elliot: Joyful Surrender
Eric Liddell: Something Greater Than Gold
Florence Young: Mission Accomplished
Francis Asbury: Circuit Rider
George Müller: The Guardian of Bristol's Orphans
Gladys Aylward: The Adventure of a Lifetime
Hudson Taylor: Deep in the Heart of China
Ida Scudder: Healing Bodies, Touching Hearts
Isobel Kuhn: On the Roof of the World
Jacob DeShazer: Forgive Your Enemies
Jim Elliot: One Great Purpose
John Flynn: Into the Never Never
John Wesley: The World His Parish
John Williams: Messenger of Peace
Jonathan Goforth: An Open Door in China
Klaus-Dieter John: Hope in the Land of the Incas
Lillian Trasher: The Greatest Wonder in Egypt
Loren Cunningham: Into All the World
Lottie Moon: Giving Her All for China

Mary Slessor: Forward into Calabar
Mildred Cable: Through the Jade Gate
Nate Saint: On a Wing and a Prayer
Paul Brand: Helping Hands
Rachel Saint: A Star in the Jungle
Rowland Bingham: Into Africa's Interior
Samuel Zwemer: The Burden of Arabia
Sundar Singh: Footprints Over the Mountains
Wilfred Grenfell: Fisher of Men
William Booth: Soup, Soap, and Salvation
William Carey: Obliged to Go

Heroes of History

by Janet & Geoff Benge

Abraham Lincoln: A New Birth of Freedom
Alan Shepard: Higher and Faster
Ben Carson: A Chance at Life
Benjamin Franklin: Live Wire
Billy Graham: America's Pastor
Captain John Smith: A Foothold in the New World
Christopher Columbus: Across the Ocean Sea
Clara Barton: Courage under Fire
Daniel Boone: Frontiersman
Davy Crockett: Ever Westward
Douglas MacArthur: What Greater Honor
Elizabeth Fry: Angel of Newgate
George Washington: True Patriot
George Washington Carver: From Slave to Scientist
Harriet Tubman: Freedombound
John Adams: Independence Forever
Laura Ingalls Wilder: A Storybook Life
Louis Zamperini: Redemption
Meriwether Lewis: Off the Edge of the Map
Milton Hershey: More Than Chocolate
Orville Wright: The Flyer
Ronald Reagan: Destiny at His Side
Theodore Roosevelt: An American Original
Thomas Edison: Inspiration and Hard Work
William Bradford: Plymouth's Rock